The Secret to a Long and Happy Life

Discover Your Ikigai

K. LOGANATHAN

Dedicated to

This book is dedicated to all young minds who pick up this book, thank you for giving my words a chance.

I want to dedicate this book to my family and friends who supported me throughout my life.

I want to dedicate this book to my English school teacher Susan Madam who motivated me and made me know my strengths.

About the Author

Born and brought up in a small village near Kalpakkam, Chennai, Loganathan did his schooling in Kendriya Vidyalaya. He holds a master's degree in physics. He has 25 years of experience in book and journal publishing. He is an experienced project manager, production editor, managing editor, Six Sigma black belt-trained quality manager, blog writer, content marketer, and trainer in publishing. He has worked with leading publishers like Wiley, Elsevier, Springer, Taylor & Francis, and other self-publishers.

You can stay connected with him on his social media handles:

 https://www.youtube.com/@logukandan6599

 www.linkedin.com/in/loganathan-k-382ba619

 https://www.instagram.com/logujay_1176/

 logusps1999@gmail.com

 https://bluegallerypublishing.mydurable.com/

Table of Contents

About the Book

Have you ever wondered what the secret is to living a long, happy, and fulfilling life? You're not alone. For centuries, people have searched for the keys to health, joy, and purpose. While there are no shortcuts or simple formulas, an ancient Japanese philosophy may point us in the right direction. It's called Ikigai.

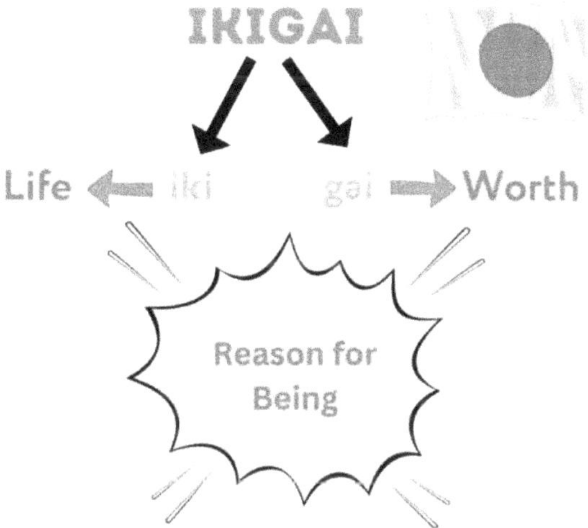

Ikigai (pronounced "e-key-gaa-e") is all about discovering your unique "reason for being." By aligning your daily life with your passions, talents, values, and sense of purpose, you cultivate the fertile soil for deep contentment and life satisfaction to bloom. This book explores the timeless wisdom of Ikigai and provides practical strategies for integrating its principles into your lifestyle.

At its heart, Ikigai teaches us to live each day feeling energized, joyful, and purposeful. It's the intersection of doing what you love, doing what you're good at, doing what the world needs, and getting compensated for your efforts. Discovering and wholeheartedly inhabiting your Ikigai allows you to wake up enthused to engage in meaningful work that positively impacts others. You experience the profound fulfillment of expressing your unique gifts and talents while contributing something of value.

> Don't worry about being successful but work toward being significant and the success will naturally follow. – Oprah Winfrey

One of Ikigai's core premises is that nurturing your sense of purpose and appreciation for life's simple joys is the secret to lasting well-being and resilience through all of life's ups and downs. This book will guide you through cultivating daily habits like mindfulness, savoring modest pleasures, and pursuing growth to continually nourish your Ikigai. You'll learn how to integrate purpose-driven routines and optimize your living spaces to inspire your reason for being.

Whether you're in your 20s, 60s or any age in between, the teachings of Ikigai contain profound insights into living with authenticity and creating the conditions for a truly satisfying life. Maybe you'll relate to the desire to feel more engagement and aliveness in your work. Perhaps you crave more balance between ambition and appreciating each day's simple gifts. Or maybe you're yearning to uncover your unique strengths and how you're meant to contribute something special.

No matter your current circumstances, Ikigai shines a light on how to live radiantly from that sacred place of purpose, meaning, and joy. Instead of deferring fulfillment to some distant future goal, it's about inhabiting every present moment as a miracle and opening yourself to your fullest potential right now.

With its origins tracing back to Okinawa, one of the regions known for producing the longest-living and most content populations, Ikigai is a reminder that lasting health and happiness flow from doing what sets your soul on fire. This book will be your guide to stepping onto the path of self-discovery, self-acceptance, mindful presence, and profound appreciation for the extraordinary gift of being alive.

Get ready to unearth your unique reason for being and learn how to weave the life-affirming practices of Ikigai into your daily routine. A whole new world of contentment, resilience, and purposeful living awaits!

Preface

Have you ever felt like something vital is missing from your life, despite checking all the boxes of success? You have a great job, a nice home, and loving family and friends. But you can't shake this nagging feeling that there has to be more to it all: more fulfillment, more joy, more purpose.

If so, you're not alone. So many of us go through life feeling discontented and disconnected, despite outward appearances. We chase ambitions, earn more money, and accumulate possessions, but it never quite fills the void inside. Our souls yearn for something deeper - a reason for being that ignites our passion and charges us with energy and authenticity.

This universal longing is what led me to the transformative philosophy of Ikigai, an ancient Japanese concept that is capturing people's imagination around the world. Ikigai (pronounced "e-key-gaa-e") translates to "a reason for being." Finding your Ikigai is the path to happiness, fulfillment, and living a life charged with energy, joy, and meaning.

The wisdom of Ikigai originates in Okinawa, one of the places where people have traditionally lived the longest, healthiest, and most satisfied lives. The philosophy's principles of cultivating purpose, resilience, presence, and treasuring life's simple pleasures provide a universal roadmap to thriving. But it's not just about longevity - Ikigai offers profound insights into how to truly live each day with vitality and contentment.

I first encountered Ikigai several years ago, and I was immediately drawn to its elegant simplicity and life-affirming essence. As someone who had checked all the boxes for "success" but still felt something missing inside, Ikigai permitted me to realign my priorities with what mattered most to me. Through embracing this new lens on life, I've been able to live with more joy, purpose, and gratitude each day.

If you find yourself nodding in recognition, then this book is for you. I share the immense wisdom of Ikigai, breaking it down into simple, accessible language with practical strategies for integrating it into your lifestyle. To live your Ikigai is to experience the profound fulfillment, happiness, and longevity that arise from wholeheartedly inhabiting your reason for being.

Whether you're at the peak of your career, contemplating retirement, or at any stage of life's journey, the teachings of Ikigai contain the seeds of possibility for revitalizing your existence. This ancient yet radically modern way of living is a call to realign yourself with your authenticity, to shed inessential burdens, and to make every day a celebration of your unique spark of brilliance.

I invite you now to dive into the magic and timeless resonance of Ikigai. May its wisdom serve as a guiding light, illuminating your path to joyful longevity, life-affirming purpose, and a deep homecoming to your most fulfilled, radiant self. Get ready to discover the secrets to wholeheartedly living your "reason for being."!

K. LOGANATHAN

1/5/2024

Who Should Read This Book?

This book on Ikigai can help many different people. But it will speak to you if any of these are true:

You feel like you're just going through the motions in life. You have a good job, a nice house, a family. But something is missing deep down. No matter what you achieve, you don't feel truly satisfied. If this sounds familiar, Ikigai can reignite your passion and make you excited about living again.

You're going through a major life change. Maybe you just graduated, started a new career, got married, had a baby, or retired. Big changes like these make us question our deeper purpose. If you're in the midst of a life transition and searching for answers, Ikigai can provide clarity.

You want to feel more engaged in your daily life. Does it feel like you're just sleepwalking through each day, mindlessly checking tasks off? This book will wake you up by helping you get clear on what truly fascinates you. Even small, boring tasks become interesting when connected to your authentic self.

You crave more balance and want to enjoy simple pleasures. Our culture pushes us to be busy and buy lots of stuff. It's easy to forget what matters. Ikigai will teach you to slow down, savor modest daily joys like a pretty sunset, and find harmony between your priorities.

You want to impact the world positively. Deep down, we all want to contribute something meaningful that helps others.

Ikigai gives you a way to purposefully use your unique skills and talents to make the world a little bit better.

You need resilience to deal with life's challenges. Whether it's loss, health issues, money problems or just feeling stuck, Ikigai will help you bounce back stronger. By connecting to your deepest purpose, you'll develop mental fortitude.

You sense untapped potential within yourself. No matter your age, Ikigai invites you to move past self-limiting beliefs and become your most authentic self. It's about staying humble, curious, and open to continual growth.

You want better overall wellness. At its core, Ikigai helps you thrive in mind, body, heart, and spirit. By realigning with your purpose, you'll naturally start taking better care of yourself too.

You want to feel more appreciation and joy in daily life. One of Ikigai's great gifts is cultivating gratitude for every passing moment. As you discover your unique reason for being, ordinary routines become filled with wonder and fulfillment.

If you nodded along to any of those, then get ready! The wisdom and practices in this book can transform how you experience your precious life. Your Ikigai journey awaits!

Chapter 1: Understanding Ikigai

Source: Canva

In today's busy world, it's so easy to get caught up chasing money, status, and success. We work hard for promotions, high pay, and fancy things. But often we forget what truly makes us happy and fulfilled deep down. This is where the beautiful Japanese idea of Ikigai can help guide us to a more meaningful life.

What is Ikigai?

"Ikigai" (生き甲斐) is a Japanese word. The closest appropriate English translation for the word "Ikigai" is "reason for being." It is pronounced "e-key-gaa-e" (ekeygaae). In Japanese, the word is a compound of "ikiru" (生きる),

which means "to live" or "to exist," and "kai" (甲斐), which means "worth," "value," or "reward," but also "fruitful" and "worth doing."

The Japanese language is richer and more open to interpretation than Western languages. Therefore, "Ikigai" has more than one meaning. From the above definitions alone, we could interpret it as "life purpose," "value of life," "fruits of life," "reward for existing," and more.

It represents the point where four important things come together: what you love, what you're good at, what the world needs, and what you can be paid for. Ikigai is about finding joy and satisfaction in the things you do every day.

Imagine waking up excited because your work combines your interests, skills, helping others, and earning a living - this is Ikigai. It's about having harmony between what you enjoy, what you do best, making the world better, and getting paid. When these pieces fit together perfectly, you live with real purpose and meaning.

The History of Ikigai

The idea of Ikigai comes from the island of Okinawa in Japan. People there have traditionally lived very long, happy lives. The Okinawan people believe that having a strong sense of Ikigai is the key to their remarkable health and contentment.

This ancient philosophy has inspired people all over the world who want to live with more joy, purpose and fulfillment in their daily lives.

The Four Components of Ikigai

What you love (Passion): These are activities, hobbies, or passions that bring you true happiness and excitement. It's about doing what you really enjoy.

What the world needs (Mission): Your mission is your purpose in life. It is the reason why you exist and what you want to achieve in the world. Your mission could be to help others, to make a positive impact on society.

What you're good at (Vocation): We all have natural talents and abilities that we're skilled at. Focusing on what you're good at gives you a sense of pride and accomplishment.

What you can be paid for (Profession): Your profession is your career or job. It is what you do to earn a living. Your profession may or may not be the same as your vocation.

Source: Canva

Imagine a Venn diagram where 'doing what you love,' 'what you are good at,' 'what the world needs,' and 'what you can be paid for' intersect. It's precisely where these four elements overlap that you'll discover your own unique Ikigai - your special reason for being that fills you with purpose, energy and joy.

Benefits of Ikigai Life

The following are the benefits of living a life with Ikigai:

1. Greater Happiness and Fulfillment: Having a strong sense of Ikigai can make your life happy and fulfilled. You have a clear sense of purpose and direction, which gives you a meaningful life.

2. Improved Physical Health: Research has shown that people who have a strong sense of purpose and meaning in life are more likely to have a better physical health. They are less likely to suffer from diseases like heart disease and stroke, and are more likely to live longer and healthy.

3. Increased Resilience: Living a life with Ikigai can help you build resilience and cope with difficult situations. When you have a clear sense of purpose and direction, you are better able to handle setbacks and challenges. You are more likely to bounce back from adversity and maintain a positive outlook in life.

4. Better Mental Health: Having a strong sense of Ikigai can also improve your mental health. It can reduce symptoms of anxiety and depression.

5. Increased Motivation and Productivity. Living a life with Ikigai can also increase your motivation and productivity. When you have a clear sense of purpose and direction, you are more likely to be focused and driven in your work and personal life. You are also more likely to be proactive and take initiative in pursuing your goals and passions.

6. Greater Sense of Connection and Community: With Ikigai life, you can build a strong connection with others and feel a greater sense of community. You are more likely to seek out like-mined individual and form a meaningful relationships.

Conclusion

Ikigai is much more than just a nice idea. It's an invitation to slow down, figure out what's truly important to you, and make sure your daily life reflects that. By embracing Ikigai values, you open up a world where every day is filled with passion, using your talents, helping others and getting paid for it.

As you start living your Ikigai, you'll find happiness in the simple joys of life. Ikigai reminds us that lasting contentment isn't about money or possessions, but doing what energizes your mind, body and spirit while making the world better. It's the path to waking up every morning with a smile, knowing you're living your unique purpose.

Chapter 2: Discovering Your Passion

The first pillar of Ikigai is passion - activities, interests, and pursuits that deeply excite and energize you. Passion provides the vital spark that animates your journey and compels you to grow. Without it, even the most ostensibly ideal mission, vocation, or profession will feel hollow and unsustainable.

Separating Real Passion from Conditioning

Sadly, many of us have lost touch with our authentic passions, buried under years of social conditioning about what we "should" enjoy based on gender roles, cultural expectations, familial pressure, and status symbols. We're taught to pursue prestige, money, and outward measures of success, rather than exploring what truly resonates with our souls.

Reclaiming your passion requires questioning every assumption you've internalized about your interests and sides. You must shed the voices of parents, teachers, peers, and media that encouraged you to pour energy into things you were told mattered, rather than what felt intrinsically vitalizing.

Unearthing Your Childhood Curiosities

One powerful way to rediscover your passions is to revisit the activities, subjects, and questions that entranced you as a child before you inherited the cynicism and responsibilities of adulthood. What filled you with insatiable curiosity and flow? What inspired you to eagerly learn and create? Might those seminal interests contain clues to your deepest motivations?

> "Passion is lifted from the earth itself by
> the muddy hands of the young; it travels
> along grass-stained sleeves to the heart."
> — Richard Louv

Experiment and Explore

Of course, some flexibility is required - rigid fixation on childhood fascinations could be limiting. You've inevitably evolved, with new experiences shifting your perspectives and expanding your mind. Approach your passion search with a beginner's mindset, permitting yourself to explore new domains that appeal to you now.

Experiment with different hobbies, classes, media, and communities. Note what engages your concentration so profoundly that hours pass like minutes. Identify what problems or questions set your mind racing with possible solutions and rabbit holes to explore further.

Honor Your Multitudes

While Ikigai emphasizes finding a harmonized life path, your passions need not be unidimensional. Humans are multifaceted beings. You may discover not one but several strands of passion that collectively comprise your motivational core. The key is honoring the breadth of your curiosities without fragmenting your focus entirely.

Conclusion

With patience, self-compassion and a commitment to self-discovery, you can begin to gain clarity on the unique drives that make you come alive. Only by unearthing this passion can you progress towards aligning all elements of your Ikigai.

Chapter 3: Identifying Your Mission

After discovering the passions that energize you, the next step in the Ikigai journey is identifying your core mission - the overarching purpose that guides your life's direction. This is the second pillar that aligns with passion for creating a harmonious sense of Ikigai.

More Than Just Work

Many people mistakenly think their mission simply equates to their job or career. But your true mission transcends any single role or path - it represents your reason for being. It's the underlying motivation that persists through all of life's ups and downs.

Your mission provides the "why" that pushes you forward, even when facing major obstacles or setbacks. While your vocation may change over time, an authentic mission remains steady as your lodestar.

Your Intended Impact

One way to get at your mission is to envision the positive impact you want to have on the world. What values, wisdom, or change do you wish to contribute that could make things better? What societal problems or injustices ignite a fire in you to take action?

Your mission could involve creating, teaching, connecting, protecting, serving, or any number of driving aims. The critical factor is that it extends beyond just personal gratification to make a difference.

> "He who has a why to live for can bear almost any how." — Friedrich Nietzsche

Sources of Profound Meaning

To uncover your unique mission, reflect deeply on experiences or beliefs that have imbued your life with a profound sense of meaning and purpose. Perhaps it was an influential mentor, philosophical text, or witnessing someone selflessly devoted to a greater cause.

Identify the undercurrent of significance and aim to distill it into a concise statement capturing the essence of your life's intended devotion. This statement can serve as a guiding light.

Prepare for Evolution

As you grow and gain new experiences, your core mission will likely evolve over time. What feels unshakable today may shift as your perspectives expand. Maintain an open, beginner's mindset to continually re-evaluate your direction.

Conclusion

The process of uncovering and committing to an overarching mission can be psychologically intense, forcing you to grapple with existential questions our society often ignores. But doing this vital inner work allows your efforts to align with lasting purpose.

Chapter 4: Aligning Your Work with Purpose

With a grasp on your core passions and higher mission, we now turn to the third pillar of Ikigai - aligning your day-to-day work and professional path with your sense of purpose. For many, this represents the biggest challenge in achieving an integrated, meaningful life.

The Unfulfilling Job Trap
In our economically driven world, millions of people find themselves stuck in jobs completely disconnected from their

innermost values and callings. Perhaps the work pays the bills but lacks any deeper resonance. Or maybe the field was chosen based on external pressures like parental expectations or status considerations rather than genuine passion.

Over time, this disconnects breeds resentment, cynicism, and emotional distress. You begin sacrificing more and more of your finite life force in service of duties that don't nourish your soul. A mundane grind replaces any sense of actively contributing value aligned with your purpose.

When Passion Meets Profit

Ideally, your profession should represent the confluence of your intrinsic motivations and the means to provide a comfortable living. When you've achieved this harmonious balance, your work takes on profound dimensions of satisfaction. Every task and project allow you to express your unique brilliance in a way that resonates with your deeper values.

Rather than compartmentalized into a "work self" and "home self", you can simply show up as your authentic, integrated self across all contexts. Productivity and creativity soar from this coherent state.

> "Nothing is as important as passion. No matter what you want to do with your life, be passionate" — Jon Bon Jovi

Reframing Income Streams

For some, aligning their literal job with purpose may not be immediately feasible. You may need to adopt a revised framework about how you generate income and view different revenue streams.

Perhaps your job simply provides a reliable baseline of income to sustain you while leaving adequate time and energy to pursue passion projects or volunteering aligned with your mission. Or maybe you're able to carve out an alternative career path that blends profit generation with purpose-driven work through entrepreneurship or self-employment.

The key is creative problem-solving to stop treating income as completely separate from purpose. Look for opportunities to harmonize the two wherever possible.

Iterative Experimentation

Very few people seamlessly align work with purpose on the first attempt. Expect to constantly iterate, try new roles and opportunities, and evolve your next moves as you gain more life experience. With patience, beginner's mindset, and commitment to self-discovery, the ideal vocation will eventually reveal itself.

Conclusion

Living in accordance with Ikigai isn't an all-or-nothing game. Each step you take towards integrated purpose and mindful work is worth celebrating. Stay resilient through the challenges - you're doing incredibly important inner work.

Chapter 5: Finding the Work You Were Born to Do

Building on aligning your profession with purpose, the fourth pillar of Ikigai involves discovering your true vocation - the type of work that allows you to contribute your unique gifts in service of something greater. This goes beyond just a job that pays the bills to a deeper calling that unlocks profound fulfillment.

Differentiate Vocation from Career

A common hurdle is conflating vocation with career. A career is simply the path you take to earn a living, oftentimes chosen based on pragmatic factors like salary potential or societal prestige. In contrast, vocation represents the work that resonates at a soul level - the labor that allows self-expression of your innate talents and driving sense of mission.

You may have had many different career iterations, but ideally, your vocation remains constant as the channel for you to offer your highest contribution to the world. When operating from this state, even menial tasks take on layers of satisfaction.

Discovering Your Innate Brilliance

So how do you identify your unique vocation? Start by looking at the natural inclinations and strengths you've demonstrated since childhood. What activities did you seem to take to effortlessly while others struggled? What modes of creative expression felt most intuitive and unlocked a sense of flow?

These clues can help uncover the inherent aptitudes and passions you were born to cultivate into mastery and offering to the world. Don't discount these impulses just because society didn't deem them "practical" - many of history's great innovators harnessed their childlike curiosity and creativity.

> "The two most important days in your life are the day you are born and the day you find out why." — Mark Twain.

Embracing Alternative Paths

For those feeling forced into a conventional career ill-suited to their vocation, technology and changing societal norms have opened new avenues. With some creative thinking and courage to buck the system, you can fashion alternative paths more aligned with your raison d'etre.

From freelancing to entrepreneurship to creative services and trades, limitless possibilities exist to design purposeful work outside the corporate mainstream. Or perhaps your vocation is more oriented towards civic engagement, activism, coaching or volunteerism. Getting resourceful often reveals viable options aligned with personal truth.

A Lifetime of Learning

Uncovering and walking the path of your vocation is not an instantaneous process, but rather a lifelong journey of growth, upskilling and refinement. You'll constantly be exposed to new knowledge, perspectives and surprise callings that could shift your trajectory.

Conclusion

The key is to embrace beginner's mindset and consistently re-evaluate whether you're still operating from your deepest place of resonance and aligned contribution. When you finally unlock this state of coherence, every day takes on profound dimensions of meaning.

Chapter 6: Exploring the Foundations of Happiness

While the first four pillars of Ikigai involve discovering your motivations and purpose, the next step is cultivating the awareness and intentionality required to actually integrate and live that purpose daily.

All humans want happiness. However, it is difficult to discover in our fast-paced, modern world. We chase achievements, material possessions, and societal milestones, but find ourselves still feeling unsatisfied. This is where the profound wisdom of Ikigai provides a path to rediscovering authentic, lasting happiness from the inside out. By aligning our daily actions with our deepest values, passions, and desire to contribute to the greater good, we open the door to true contentment and joy.

The Connection Between Ikigai and Happiness

Have you ever noticed how some people just seem to radiate joy and contentment, even when life gets difficult? The secret to their happiness likely lies in living with Ikigai - having a strong sense of purpose and meaning. Ikigai provides the foundation for true, lasting happiness.

When your daily activities line up with your values, interests, talents and desire to be paid for your efforts, you cultivate an extremely positive outlook. Doing work that energizes you, using your natural skills, helping society, and earning money creates deep fulfillment. This powerful combination fills you with optimism, gratitude, and satisfaction - the core ingredients for genuine happiness.

Finding Joy in Everyday Life

While major life goals like getting married, buying a home, or traveling the world can provide an initial thrill, true happiness comes from the little things we experience day to day. Ikigai teaches us to slow down and savor life's simple joys like a delicious meal, a warm sunny day, or an enjoyable conversation with friends.

When you live guided by your Ikigai, you bring more consciousness to routine tasks and encounters. You feel a childlike sense of wonder seeing a colorful sunrise, hearing a beautiful song, or smelling freshly baked bread. With an Ikigai mindset, the ordinary becomes extraordinary as you view the world through fresh, appreciative eyes.

Cultivating Gratitude and Appreciation

A key part of Ikigai is focusing on what you already have, instead of pining for more money, possessions or success. Through the practice of gratitude, you feel thankful for your interests, abilities, relationships, accomplishments, and the beauty around you. You develop a deep appreciation for life's bounties.

Adopting an attitude of gratitude has been proven to increase happiness and life satisfaction. When you approach each day with Ikigai, you feel genuinely grateful to use your talents to help others and do work you find meaningful. This perspective nurtures optimism, positive moods and overall well-being.

Conclusion

Living with Ikigai allows you to make the most of each precious day. You wake up with a sense of purpose, savoring life's joys, cultivating gratitude, and radiating authentic happiness from the inside out.

Chapter 7: Finding Balance and Harmony

In our achievement-obsessed culture, it's all too easy to slip into a cycle of overworking, negative stress, and personal neglect – leaving us feeling burnt out, unhappy, and disconnected from what truly matters. The philosophy of Ikigai acts as a powerful counterweight, guiding us back toward balance, harmony, and inner peace. By being more present, nurturing our relationships, and flowing with life's natural rhythms, we can create the conditions for sustainable well-being and fulfillment.

Striking a Balance Between Work and Leisure

In our always-on, hustle culture it's far too easy to become consumed by work and professional ambitions. But living with Ikigai means striving for balance between our careers and making time for rest, recreation and leisure activities we enjoy.

Having a fulfilling job that aligns with your values and talents is immensely rewarding. But Ikigai reminds us that true happiness also requires unplugging from work to recharge our minds and bodies. Make time for hobbies like reading, gardening or playing sports. Prioritize quality downtime with loved ones. This balance allows you to be more present, engaged, and satisfied in all areas of life.

Creating Harmony in Relationships

Healthy, loving relationships are central to our well-being and happiness. From romantic partners to family, friends and colleagues, nurturing positive connections creates harmony in our lives. Ikigai provides a framework for building understanding and bringing our best selves to our relationships.

With an Ikigai mindset, we listen deeply, express gratitude and seek to add value through our talents and abilities. We spend quality time pursuing mutually enjoyable interests. We repair conflicts through open and honest dialogue. And we uplift each other in serving our shared purpose. Bringing these Ikigai principles to our relationships cultivates trust, care, and enduring bonds.

Finding Peace Amidst Chaos

Let's face it, modern life can feel overwhelming at times with constant demands, distractions, and stressors coming our way.

Having a well-defined Ikigai provides an anchoring sense of clarity and calm amidst the whirlwind.

When you live guided by your reason for being, you develop the ability to remain grounded and focused on what matters most. You view challenges as opportunities to apply your strengths. You rally your energy towards meaningful pursuits. And you consciously make space for restorative self-care activities like spending time in nature, meditating or journaling. This mindful presence allows you to move through turbulence with greater ease and inner peace.

Conclusion

True balance is not about glossing over difficulties or avoiding life's inevitable stresses, but rather developing the resilience and presence of mind to navigate challenges with more ease and grace. Ikigai provides a roadmap for restoring harmony – reminding us to replenish our energy through joyful pursuits, foster loving connections, and remain anchored in our core purpose and values. With the equilibrium cultivated through living an Ikigai life, we become better equipped to roll with life's ups and downs while sustained by an underlying sense of contentment.

Chapter 8: Nurturing Health and Wellness

When we consider how to live a truly meaningful and fulfilling life aligned with Ikigai, nurturing our health and well-being is an essential foundation. After all, we need abundant physical, mental, and spiritual energy to be able to wholeheartedly pursue our passions, share our talents with the world, and experience deep personal growth along the way. From this holistic perspective rooted in ancient Japanese wisdom, vibrant well-being allows us to thrive as fully expressed human beings.

The Importance of Physical Health

While Ikigai is focused on finding purpose and cultivating joy, it's impossible to truly thrive without taking care of our physical health and well-being. When our bodies feel energized and strong, we have more vigor to pursue our passions and serve the world in a bigger way.

An Ikigai lifestyle encourages nourishing our bodies through balanced nutrition, ample hydration, regular exercise, and high-quality sleep. Approach these pillars of health not from a punishing perspective, but from a sense of commitment to fueling your abilities to live your purpose fully. Small, sustainable steps like drinking more water, walking daily, and prioritizing rest go a long way.

Nourishing Your Mind and Soul

While tending to our physical vessel is vital, Ikigai reminds us to nurture our psychological, emotional and spiritual well-being too. Our mindset, creativity, and sense of wonder are precious resources to be exercised and replenished.

Feed your mind through avenues like reading, taking a class, listening to podcasts or having stimulating conversations. Express your emotions through journaling, art or simply talking things out with a loved one. Nurture your soul through practices like meditation, spending time in nature, or exploring your spiritual beliefs. This holistic self-care allows your whole self to feel energized and thriving.

Embracing Holistic Wellness Practices

From the Japanese tradition itself, Ikigai is inherently a holistic philosophy recognizing we must care for our multidimensional mind-body-spirit needs. Many traditional wellness practices can support living an Ikigai-aligned life.

For example, yoga combines physical postures, breathwork, meditation, and spiritual study into one integrated practice. Japanese traditions like forest bathing (shinrin-yoku), intentional aloness (morita), and expressions of wabi-sabi beauty and impermanence invite harmony between self and nature. An Ikigai lifestyle celebrates a holistic approach to well-being.

Conclusion

In many ways, an Ikigai lifestyle is one of conscious self-care and nourishment at every level – body, mind, heart, and spirit. By committing to proactive wellness practices, we awaken our full vitality to be able to truly soar in living our reason for being. At the same time, caring for our holistic health allows us to move through life's challenges with more grit and grace. Ultimately, nurturing our multi-dimensional well-being creates the fertile inner soil for our Ikigai to blossom in beautiful, life-affirming ways.

Chapter 9: Embracing Self-Discovery and Reflection

At the heart of the Ikigai philosophy lies a call to embark discovery journey of honest self-exploration. Only by cultivating a deep understanding of our authentic selves – our core values, innate gifts, and what ignites our passion – can we hope to uncover our unique reason for being. This chapter invites you to slow down, go inward, and engage in the brave work of self-discovery and reflection. It is in these profound moments of personal insight that we awaken to our true potential and pave the way for living with purpose.

Cultivating Self-Awareness

Self-awareness is like an inward-facing flashlight, illuminating the depths of our psyche. By getting curious about our thoughts, emotions, beliefs, and behaviors, we reveal our unconscious drivers and motivations. This awareness empowers us to make conscious choices aligned with our Ikigai.

Practices like mindfulness meditation, journaling, and simply listening to our inner voice all support heightened self-knowledge. We learn our authentic preferences rather than going along with societal expectations. We identify core values like creativity, service, or freedom. We understand our personal strengths and growth areas. This clarity creates the foundation for an Ikigai-aligned life.

Reflecting on Your Life's Purpose

At the very center of Ikigai lies the quest to discover your life's unique purpose – the particular way you feel called to contribute to society and the legacy you wish to create. This driving sense of personal mission provides trajectory and inspiration for living meaningfully.

Explore what issues you feel passionate about solving. What skills or life experiences equip you to serve distinctively? How might you combine your talents to innovate or inspire? Courageously turn inward and allow your deepest longings for purpose to arise and take shape.

Embracing Vulnerability and Growth

The journey of self-discovery is not always easy – it requires vulnerability, humility, and a willingness to be honest about our fears and shortcomings. But this is fertile ground for immense growth and personal transformation.

Have the courage to examine your limiting beliefs, insecurities, and hidden emotional patterns. Extract wisdom from past failures or stagnant periods. Be willing to course-correct, abandon what's not serving you, and lean into newfound insights about your gifts and callings. This intentional self-reflection and change unleash continual rebirth toward more authentic self-expression.

Conclusion

While the self-discovery process can feel daunting at times, it is an invaluable investment in understanding and unleashing your unique brilliance. For how can you hope to experience the fulfillment of living your Ikigai if you don't first get radically honest about who you are at the core?

Commit to this inner work with patience and self-compassion. Trust that wisdom awaits your curiosity, and profound awakenings lie on the other side of vulnerability. By shining light on your innermost self – strengths, passions, growth edges and all – the path for expressing your reason for being becomes illume. From this place of deep self-knowledge, you can fully embrace the journey of Ikigai.

Chapter 10: Pursuing Personal Growth and Self-Improvement

The quest to live a life of Ikigai – infused with passion, purpose, and fulfillment – is an ever-evolving journey of continual growth and self-actualization. As we deepen our self-knowledge and align with our unique reason for being, we encounter new expansion opportunities. This chapter explores how to actively pursue your potential through practices like goal-setting, shedding limiting beliefs and embracing lifelong learning. By committing to your personal development, you create fertile soil for your Ikigai to flourish.

Setting Goals and Taking Action

Once you identify areas of interest or growth desires, it's essential to cultivate the ability to transform visions into reality through concrete goal-setting and committed action. Give your Ikigai traction by breaking down larger aspirations into achievable, incremental steps.

Perhaps you wish to change careers, launch an entrepreneurial venture, or develop a new skill. Establish clear, time-bound objectives. Outline practical action plans. Celebrate small wins along the way to build momentum. Taking purposeful action, consistently over time, allows you to actively manifest facets of your Ikigai.

Overcoming Limiting Beliefs

We all hold unconscious limiting beliefs that can stunt our growth and self-expression. Outdated narratives about our capabilities, self-worth, or what's possible. The self-reflection practices of Ikigai provide opportunities to shine a light on these self-imposed constraints.

Identify and question the origin of beliefs holding you back, replacing them with personal affirmations rooted in self-belief. Visualize yourself already embodying the version of you, you aspire to become. Courageously confront inner critics and naysayers with conviction in your potential. Dismantling limitations clears space to more boldly pursue your Ikigai.

Continuing Education and Learning

An Ikigai mindset is one of humble curiosity and receptiveness to continual learning and skill expansion. You understand your reason for being is a lifelong process of growth and mastery. Approach life as an eternal student.

Take workshops related to your interests or entrepreneurial
visions. Read works by thought-leaders in your fields of
passion. Find mentors and join communities oriented around
your purposeful pursuits. Not only do you gain practical
knowledge, but you cultivate an inspired, ever-evolving
perspective essential to living your Ikigai wholeheartedly.

Conclusion

At its core, Ikigai is a perpetual practice of personal growth –
becoming more fully expressed versions of ourselves, with
unique gifts ablaze. By setting intention, taking action,
challenging limiting beliefs, and embracing education, we
engage our utmost potential.

Living our reason for being is not a static state, but an
ongoing co-creative process of evolution and self-
actualization. Lean into this expansion with curiosity and faith
in your infinite ability to positively transform. For growth
itself, and all it allows you to give to the world, becomes a
meditation on your Ikigai.

Chapter 11: Cultivating Inner Harmony

In a world that constantly bombards us with noise, distractions, and demands on our time and energy, it's easy to feel overwhelmed and disconnected from our innermost selves. Yet the philosophy of Ikigai teaches us that to truly live with purpose and fulfillment, we must cultivate a deep sense of inner harmony – a state of tranquility, balance, and alignment within our minds, bodies, and souls. This chapter explores powerful practices for quieting the external chaos and nurturing the sacred refuge of peace that resides within each of us.

Finding Peace Within

At the core of inner harmony lies the ability to access a state of inner peace and presence, even amidst life's inevitable storms. Practices like meditation, breathwork, and gentle moving meditations like yoga or qigong allow us to turn our attention inward, calming the turbulence of an overactive mind.

As you commit to these grounding rituals, you develop the skill of witnessing your thoughts and emotions with non-judgmental awareness, rather than being consumed by them. You create space to reconnect with your innate sense of wholeness and wisdom. From this still point of presence, you can respond to situations with greater clarity and wisdom.

Practicing Self-Compassion

So often, we are our own harshest critics – berating ourselves over perceived flaws, failures, or missteps. This inner voice of negativity builds unhealthy stress and disharmony within. Ikigai encourages us to transform this pattern by treating ourselves with compassion.

Notice and accept your inner critic without judgment, then consciously reframe those harsh inner narratives through the lens of kindness, empathy and unconditional self-acceptance. Give yourself kudos for efforts made, lessons learned, and simply showing up as a human on this journey of growth. Over time, replacing self-criticism with self-compassion soothes the internal discordance.

Letting Go of Attachments

Much of our internal dissonance stems from grasping or clinging – to material possessions, limiting beliefs, unhealthy relationships or circumstances no longer serving us. An Ikigai approach to life involves the practice of surrender and detachment.

Reflect on what you may be white-knuckling out of habit, fear or misguided control. Material items you've outgrown? Resentments or grievances poisoning your peace? Limiting stories about your possibilities? Have the courage to release these outdated attachments, allowing your mind and heart to feel lighter and more buoyant.

Conclusion

By exploring practices for inner stillness, self-compassion and surrendering attachments, we create fertile inner space for a harmonious life guided by Ikigai to bloom. From this resonant state of equilibrium within, our clarity of purpose intensifies and our ability to embrace each moment with presence blossoms.

While the outer world may always involve some level of complexity and chaos, those living their Ikigai can remain rooted in an unshakable experience of wholeness and centeredness. This inner harmony becomes the eye of the storm – providing profound nourishment to weather any external turbulence with grace, wisdom and an abiding contentment in simply being.

Chapter 12: Finding Meaning and Purpose

At the very heart of Ikigai lies the universal human longing to discover our unique sense of meaning and purpose. We all share an innate desire to feel that our lives, our efforts, and our existence truly matter in some profound way. This chapter explores how the philosophy of Ikigai can help guide us in uncovering and wholeheartedly living our deepest reasons for being.

Exploring the Quest for Meaning

From ancient times across all cultures, the great poets, philosophers and spiritual teachers have grappled with the inquiry: What is the meaning of life? While no single answer can encapsulate the richness of the human experience, Ikigai provides a powerful framework for unearthing your own personal understanding of life's significance.

By looking inward and reflecting on the ways you feel most alive and purposeful, you can start to piece together the intricate tapestry of themes, values, and callings that imbue your life with profound meaning. Perhaps it's creative self-expression, stewardship for the environment, or cultivating strong communities. Allow your heart to illuminate what ignites that vital spark of meaning within you.

Defining Your Mission

As you gain clarity around the issues and ideals that resonate most deeply, your unique personal sense of purpose starts taking shape. Ikigai encourages you to distill and articulate this driving mission into a powerfully evocative statement of intention.

What is the specific positive impact or legacy you feel called to create in the world? How might your particular gifts, experiences, and perspectives allow you to contribute something distinctive? Crafting a personal mission statement provides laser-like focus and motivation for aligning all aspects of your life in service of living this purpose wholeheartedly.

Connecting with Your Ikigai

When you synthesize your self-knowledge about what brings you joy, what you excel at, how you can be compensated, and how you can tangibly serve others, you arrive at a crystallized expression of your Ikigai – that beautiful intersection of passion, talent, fruitful labor, and purposeful contribution.

From this anchoring point of clarity, each day becomes an opportunity to live more and more in integrity with your reason for being. You make decisions and engage in activities that tangibly connect you to your purpose. Life takes on a quality of profound resonance as you exist in harmonious orbit with your Ikigai.

Conclusion

While finding one's unique meaning and purpose can seem like a lofty quest, Ikigai demonstrates that the answers lie within each of us already. By connecting inward, we can bring forth our most essential selves and motivations into full luminous expression.

Embracing the path of Ikigai provides a powerful compass for navigating this discovery process with patience, curiosity and trust in your inner voice. Have faith that the longing for purpose burning bright within you contains its own medicine for revealing your unique role to play in this human experience. As you realign with your gifts and reason for being, life unveils itself as a masterpiece imbued with sacred significance.

Chapter 13: Integrating Ikigai into Your Lifestyle

While the concepts of Ikigai can feel deeply inspiring, the real power lies in how we practically integrate and embody these principles into our daily lives. This chapter explores ways to make Ikigai not just a philosophy, but a fully engaged way of being that touches every aspect of your lifestyle. By fusing your reason for being into your routines, environments, and moment-to-moment choices, you breathe life into your Ikigai.

Making Ikigai a Daily Practice

Living your Ikigai is not a final destination to be reached, but an ever-evolving journey of small, intentional daily actions. Ask yourself each morning, "How can I align more closely with my purpose today?" Then follow through by weaving your unique reason for being into your routine.

If creative expression is part of your Ikigai, start your day writing, sketching, or coding. If community service calls you, build in time to volunteer locally. If cultivating loving relationships matters deeply, be fully present during meals with loved ones. By ritualizing Ikigai-aligned practices, you strengthen the pathways of purpose.

Creating Ikigai Rituals

In addition to your daily Ikigai actions, design larger rituals that allow you to regularly immerse yourself in the essence of your life's reason for being. These can be weekly, monthly, or annually.

An artist may take a quarterly personal retreat to focus solely on their creative work. A teacher may begin each school year by reaffirming their philosophy of education. A nature-lover might take an annual solo hiking trip to reconnect with their love of the wilderness. These rituals provide potent ways to step outside your ordinary routines and rededicate yourself to your deepest sources of meaning.

Aligning Your Environment

Just as Ikigai shapes your actions, it can also influence your physical environment and surroundings. Intentionally crafting living and working spaces that reflect and support your purpose creates powerful spaces of inspiration.

Fill your home with objects, art, books, and belongings that symbolize your Ikigai interests and values. Structure your office to optimally facilitate the type of work you find most purposeful. Even small adjustments like displaying meaningful photos or mementos can breathe more Ikigai energy into your spaces.

Conclusion

While discovering your Ikigai is a tremendous first step, it's through your daily lifestyle choices that you substantiate it into a tangible, embodied reality. As you mindfully make space for purpose-driven routines, rituals, and surroundings, your entire existence becomes a breathing expression of your reason for being.

There is profound power in fusing the lofty concepts of Ikigai into your most micro, ordinary moments - for it's the accumulation of these small acts of incarnating purpose that ultimately shapes the legacy you leave. As your lifestyle reflects your Ikigai more completely, each breath, thought and action resonate with the clarity of your deepest motivations.

Chapter 14: Sustaining Happiness and Fulfillment

Living your Ikigai isn't about short-term bursts of happiness from checking boxes or buying things. It's cultivating a deep, lasting sense of joy and satisfaction that becomes part of who you are. As you align your daily life to your unique reason for being, you tap into an endless wellspring of real contentment. This chapter explores lifestyle habits to nurture and maintain the wonderful happiness that naturally blossoms from living with purpose.

Cultivating Daily Joy

Big life events like weddings, having babies, or achieving goals can make us happy for a while. But the greatest joy comes from truly appreciating all the simple, ordinary pleasures that make up each day. When you live with an Ikigai mindset, you can find delight and wonder in the littlest things.

Wake up and feel the warm sun on your face. When eating, savor every flavor and texture of the food. During your commute, gaze at the pretty trees and buildings you pass. Pausing to be totally present and soak in these humble daily joys creates sustainable happiness.

Practicing Mindful Living

Mindfulness means being completely focused and aware on the here and now, instead of dwelling on the past or worrying about tomorrow. It allows you to fully drink in the profound fulfillment available in each second of living your reason for being.

Be mindful when doing simple routines like brushing your teeth, showering, or driving to work. When talking with others, listen attentively instead of thinking about other things. No matter how basic or boring the task, it's a chance to experience the extraordinary miracle of simply being alive and living with purpose.

Embracing the Journey

Ikigai teaches that true, lasting happiness isn't found in finally reaching a certain goal, but in embracing every single step along the path of life as a remarkable part of the journey itself.

Don't cling to how you think life, work or relationships are "supposed" to be. Stay open to how your path naturally unfolds, even when it's bumpy. See challenges as sacred opportunities to learn and grow, not frustrations. With a curious, beginner's mindset, each new day offers endless sources of happiness through living your Ikigai fully.

Conclusion

Our society tells us happiness comes from accomplishments and buying more stuff. But Ikigai reveals the deepest wellspring of joy is available right here, right now, when we're truly present and living with purpose.

By developing habits of slowing down, savoring simple pleasures, and appreciating the miracle of being alive, we nourish a profound, unshakable sense of contentment. Each moment spent purposefully pursuing our interests, nurturing our wellbeing, and connecting with our reason for being becomes a meditation on fulfillment itself. From this sacred space of inhabiting the journey, real, sustainable happiness flows freely as a natural state of grace.

Chapter 15: Sustaining Your Ikigai Journey

Discovering and aligning your life with your Ikigai - your unique reason for being - is an incredibly powerful and transformative experience. However, your Ikigai is not a final destination, but an ever-evolving journey to be nurtured and sustained throughout your lifetime. This chapter explores practices for staying steadfastly committed to living your purpose, even when confronted with obstacles, and adapting your Ikigai as your life circumstances change.

Staying Committed to Your Ikigai

No matter how much clarity you have about your life's purpose, there will inevitably be times when doubts, frustrations, or setbacks can shake your commitment and motivation. During these periods, it's vital to reconnect with the core reasons why you embarked on this Ikigai path to begin with.

Keep a journal documenting how living purposefully has enriched your life and positively impacted others. Revisit your mission statement regularly. Surround yourself with images, affirmations, and talismans that remind you of your "why." Call upon your community to provide accountability and encouragement. These practices can help reignite and sustain your Ikigai commitment.

Cultivating Resilience

The journey of Ikigai, like any worthwhile pursuit, will present its share of challenges, failures, and difficulties to overcome. That's why cultivating resilience - the ability to flexibly adapt and bounce back amidst adversity - is so essential.

Approach obstacles with curiosity rather than judgment, asking "What is this situation asking me to learn?" Maintain a growth mindset, seeing life's challenges as pathways for developing fortitude. Learn from past setbacks about managing stress and negative thought patterns. By building your resilience muscle, you'll be able to courageously keep showing up for your purpose.

Adapting Your Ikigai

While your core Ikigai will likely remain consistent, the specific outward expressions and avenues for pursuing your purpose often need to shift and evolve. Remaining rigidly attached to how you initially envisioned living your Ikigai can hinder your growth and long-term sustainability.

Perhaps your interests, skills, or circumstances have changed, calling for new creative outlets aligned with your reason for being. Or maybe new opportunities have emerged that could expand how you tangibly contribute from your Ikigai. Holding a beginner's mind and being willing to course-correct as needed allows your Ikigai to remain vitally relevant.

Your journey of Ikigai contains many chapters - times of profound inspiration, periods of struggle, pivotal moments of change, and growth. What sustains you is an unwavering commitment to your life's purpose, even when the path gets difficult.

By nurturing your "why" and drawing upon practices to cultivate resilience in the face of challenges, you strengthen your Ikigai roots. By remaining open to how your purpose naturally evolves, you allow your Ikigai expression to continually expand in alignment with your ever-unfolding human potential. Sustaining this vibrant, living connection to your reason for being is a lifelong practice of choosing to show up fully for the miraculous journey.

Chapter 16: Conclusion - Embracing the Path to Fulfillment

You've now gained a deeper understanding of the timeless Japanese philosophy of Ikigai and how to integrate its profound wisdom into your daily life. By discovering and aligning with your unique reason for being, you open yourself to experiencing true fulfillment, purpose, and sustainable happiness. As you conclude this journey, it's an opportunity to reflect on the insights that resonate most deeply and prepare to wholeheartedly embrace your Ikigai path.

Reflecting on Your Ikigai Journey

Take a few moments to pause and consider how your perspective on life's meaning and your sense of purpose may have shifted through exploring the principles of Ikigai. What new self-discoveries did you unearth about your passions, talents, and values? How might you now approach cultivating more presence, authenticity, and appreciation in your daily existence?

Bring to mind the specific lifestyle practices that felt most nourishing and natural for you to integrate - whether it was approaches to mindful living, dedicated routines for creative pursuits, acts of service, or moments savoring nature's beauty. Visualize how it will feel to steadily establish these Ikigai-aligned habits.

As you reflect, also notice any lingering doubts, resistances, or places where you may still feel "stuck." Offer yourself compassion, and trust that deeper clarity will emerge through your committed practice over time.

Sharing Your Ikigai with Others

One of the great joys of living your Ikigai is the opportunity to inspire those around you by sharing the gifts, talents, and passions that make you uniquely you. As you become more emboldened in your purpose, don't be afraid to let your light shine!

You might express your Ikigai through tangible acts of service or creating art that moves others. Or perhaps you'll find yourself sharing insights about work-life harmony or personal growth that help illuminate someone else's path. You could even gather a group to explore Ikigai principles together through study and discussion.

When we courageously show up as our authentic, purpose-driven selves, we permit others to do the same. Your committed embodiment of Ikigai becomes a living invitation to create more light.

Celebrating Your Ikigai

At every step along this journey of self-discovery, growth, and ever-deepening alignment with your reason for being, there is a profound cause for celebration! You've done the essential introspective work of unearthing your essence. You've committed to an ongoing practice of nourishing your mind, body, and spirit. You're bravely letting your unique brilliance shine in the world.

So, pause to feel gratitude for how far you've already come, and appreciate the miraculous opportunity to live this one precious life with purpose and meaning. Embrace the beauty of this awakening with humble awe and authentic joy. For you have wholeheartedly chosen to walk the path of Ikigai – a remarkable journey of fully inhabiting your reason for being each day, and leaving a radiant legacy simply through wholehearted living.

As you step forward, know that Ikigai will remain your trusted wise guide, revealing new layers of purpose, clarity, and contentment in every sacred moment. With an open heart and mind, get ready to embrace the path to fulfillment that lies joyfully before you.

Appendix A - Identify Your Ikigai Using Excel Template

In this appendix, we provide a step-by-step guide along with an Excel template to help you uncover your IKIGAI – your reason for being – using the IKIGAI framework. Follow these steps and use the provided template to gain clarity on your purpose and direction in life.

Step 1: Understand the IKIGAI Framework

Before diving into the template, let's understand the four pillars of the IKIGAI framework:

1. What you love: Your passions, hobbies, and interests.

Example: Writing poetry, playing the guitar, cooking, hiking, teaching, volunteering in animal shelters, gardening, solving puzzles, painting, etc.

2. What you are good at: Your skills, strengths, and areas of expertise.

Example: Graphic design, public speaking, programming, problem-solving, customer service, analyzing data, playing musical instruments, photography, strategic planning, etc.

3. What the world needs: Societal needs, causes, and issues that matter.

Example: Sustainable energy solutions, education for underprivileged children, mental health support, clean water access, affordable housing, healthcare services, environmental conservation, innovative technology, community building, etc.

4. What you can be paid for: Marketable skills, professions, and career opportunities.

Example: Software development, marketing consulting, financial advising, project management, event planning, content creation, healthcare services, graphic design, teaching, engineering, etc.

Combining these elements can help individuals find their purpose and direction in life. It's where passion, mission, vocation, and profession intersect. Finding the right balance between these four aspects can lead to a fulfilling and meaningful life.

Step 2: Fill Out the Template

The provided Excel template below consists of four columns: "Elements of IKIGAI," "Examples," "Importance," and "Rate." Here's how to fill it out:

1. **Elements of IKIGAI:** List the four aspects of IKIGAI – What you love, What you are good at, What the world needs, and What you can be paid for – in this column.

2. **Examples:** Provide specific examples or activities that fall under each aspect.

3. **Importance:** Assign a number from 1 to 5 to indicate the importance of each aspect to you, where 5 is the highest importance.

4. **Rate:** Rate how well you meet each aspect on a scale from 1 to 5, where 1 is the lowest and 5 is the highest.

Elements of IKIGAI	Examples	Importance	Rate
What you love	Playing guitar	5	4
What you are good at	Graphic design	4	5
What the world needs	Sustainable energy solutions	5	3
What you can be paid for	Software development	4	4

Step 3: Calculate Your IKIGAI Score

Once you've filled out the template, follow these steps to calculate your IKIGAI score:

1. For each row, multiply the Importance by the Rate to get a weighted score.

2. Then, sum up these weighted scores.

3. Divide the total by the sum of the Importance values.

4. The resulting value represents your IKIGAI score, indicating the alignment of your passions, skills, societal needs, and market opportunities.

Example of Balance Calculation:

- Weighted average = [(5*4) + (4*5) + (5*3) + (4*4)] / (5 + 4 + 5 + 4) = (20 + 20 + 15 + 16) / 18 = 71 / 18 ≈ 3.944

- So, the calculated balance is approximately 3.944.

Step 4: Interpret Your Results

Interpret your IKIGAI score to gain insights into your
purpose and direction in life:

- A score closer to 5 indicates a strong alignment with your
  IKIGAI.
- A score closer to 1 suggests a weaker alignment,
  indicating areas for improvement.

Conclusion

Uncovering your IKIGAI can lead to a more fulfilling and
purpose-driven life. Use the provided template and guide to
explore the intersection of your passions, skills, societal
needs, and market opportunities, and embark on a journey
towards a life of meaning and fulfillment.

Appendix B - Identify Your Ikigai Through Venn Diagram

In this appendix, we can see how to use a Venn diagram and understand Ikigai. We'll represent each aspect of Ikigai (What you love, What you are good at or your strengths, What the world needs, What you can be paid for) as a separate circle in the diagram. The intersection of these circles will represent where these aspects overlap (sweet spot), potentially indicating your Ikigai.

Example: Finding Ikigai through a Venn Diagram

1. Draw Four Circles:

- Draw four overlapping circles on a piece of paper or in a digital drawing tool.

2. Label Each Circle:

- Label the circles with the following aspects of Ikigai: Passion, Profession, Vocation, and Mission.

3. Fill in Examples:

- Inside each circle, write down examples that correspond to that aspect based on your love, strength, paid for, and societal needs.
- **Passion (Love):** Playing guitar, cooking, hiking
- **Profession (Strengths):** Graphic design, programming, problem-solving
- **Vocation (Paid for):** Software development, marketing consulting, financial advising
- **Mission (Societal Needs):** Sustainable energy solutions, education for underprivileged children, mental health support

4. Overlap Areas:

- Identify the overlapping areas between the circles and see how they intersect.

5. Find the Sweet Spot:

- Explore the central area where all four circles overlap. This represents your potential IKIGAI—the convergence of what you love, what you're good at, what the world needs, and what you can be paid for.

6. Example of IKIGAI Intersection:

- In the central area where all circles overlap, you might find activities or pursuits such as:

  - Developing sustainable energy solutions (Mission) through programming skills (Strength) in a career as a software developer (Paid for) while being passionate about environmental conservation (Love).

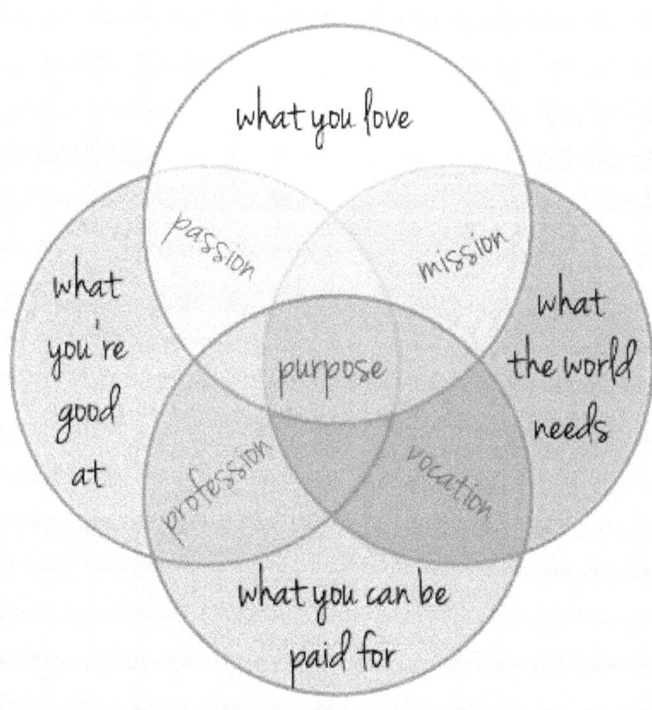

Source: https://livingtoroam.com/ikigai/

What does this mean?

Passion: The things that you love and that you're also good at.

Mission: The things that the world needs and that you also love.

Vocation: The things that you can be paid for and also that the world needs.

Profession: The things that you're good at and also what you can be paid for.

If you focus on the overlapping points, you will find yourself a lot closer to what your ikigai, your true purpose, actually is.

By following these steps and visualizing IKIGAI through a Venn diagram, you can gain a clearer understanding of how different aspects of your life intersect and where your purpose and fulfillment may lie.

References

Kindly explore the below listed resources to further enrich your exploration of Ikigai and personal development. These resources include insightful YouTube channels and informative websites that offer additional perspectives, practical tips, and inspiring content to support your journey towards discovering your purpose and living a fulfilling life.

https://www.youtube.com/watch?v=nYrB5mOh5Ag&ab_channel=BookSummaryLAB

https://www.youtube.com/watch?v=vV5OKoF1Y6Y&ab_channel=PhilosophiesforLife

https://www.youtube.com/watch?v=Zxj3P0enJNQ&ab_channel=ImprovementPill

https://www.youtube.com/watch?v=RJ5Srezh190&ab_channel=Happinesscom

https://livingtoroam.com/ikigai/ (finding your Ikigai)

https://www.youtube.com/watch?v=PQrub29_nRo&ab_channel=PrimeMinister%27sOfficeofJapan

https://biarahman.wordpress.com/2016/08/04/discover-your-ikigai/ (Ikigai worksheet)

Books By This Author

The author's first book is "Artificial Intelligence for Kids". This book is an introduction to artificial intelligence (AI). This fun book helps kids understand and use AI. The book unleashes creativity through art projects and strengthens problem-solving skills. It shows how AI has already impacted daily life and where future innovations will lead. This book is for kids, their parents, and teachers to understand how to use AI in a good way. It paperback edition was published on Notion Press including Amazon and eBook on Gumroad and Pothi.com.

Notion Press (Paperback)
https://notionpress.com/read/artifici...

Gumroad (ebook) https://logujay.gumroad.com/l/AIkids

Pothi.com (ebook) https://pothi.com/pothi/book/ebook-ka...

Amazon (paperback)

https://www.amazon.in/dp/B0CVQHGX9N?&tag=notionp com-21

The author's second book is "The 10 Biggest Career Blunders: Mistakes to Avoid for Success". This book shares the 10 MONSTROUS career mistakes that hold too many professionals back from reaching their potential. Backed by real-life stories and science-based insights, it will open your eyes to hidden pitfalls that could sabotage your efforts – also known as career killers. This book provides you with the tools to create a rewarding work life by calling out the biggest blunders ahead of time. That way you can be career thriving rather than career stifled. Time to give yourself an advantage!

The kindle edition **sold 100 units** with a **80 five stars** reviews.

https://www.amazon.in/dp/B0CTBMH8WY

The paperback versions are published in Notion Press (Indian edition) and Amazon (International edition)

https://www.amazon.com/dp/B0CWRBRTJB

https://notionpress.com/read/the-10-biggest-career-blunders